TAILS

Please visit our web site at: **www.garethstevens.com**
For a free color catalog describing Gareth Stevens Publishing's list of high-quality books and multimedia programs, call 1-800-542-2595 or fax your request to (414) 332-3567.

Library of Congress Cataloging-in-Publication Data

Whittaker, Nicola.
  [Creature tails]
  Tails / by Nicola Whittaker.
    p. cm. — (Creature features)
  Includes index.
  Summary: Simple text and photographs show many different kinds of tails and various things they can do. Includes a picture glossary which identifies the animals pictured and provides information to help with classification skills.
  ISBN 0-8368-3166-7 (lib. bdg.)
  1. Tail—Juvenile literature. [1. Tail. 2. Animals—Habits and behavior.] I. Title.
QL950.6.W55   2002
591.4—dc21   2002019521

This North American edition first published in 2002 by
Gareth Stevens Publishing
A World Almanac Education Group Company
330 West Olive Street, Suite 100
Milwaukee, Wisconsin 53212 USA

This U.S. edition © 2002 by Gareth Stevens, Inc. Original edition © 2001 by Franklin Watts. First published in 2001 by Franklin Watts, 96 Leonard Street, London WC2A 4XD, England.

Franklin Watts editor: Samantha Armstrong
Franklin Watts designer: Jason Anscomb
Science consultant: Dr. Jim Flegg

Gareth Stevens editor: Dorothy L. Gibbs
Cover design: Tammy Gruenewald

Picture credits:
NHPA: cover (James Carmichael, Jr.; Yves Lanceau; Stephen Dalton), 5 (Martin Harvey), 6-7 (A.N.T.), 8-9 (Henry Ausloos), 10 (Manfred Danegger), 11 (Stephen Dalton), 12-13 (Kevin Schafer), 16 (Andy Rouse), 17 (T. Kitchin and V. Hurst), 18-19 (Yves Lanceau), 19 (Anthony Bannister), 20-21 (Daniel Heuclin), 22-23 (Daniel Heuclin), 25 (Nigel J. Dennis).
Oxford Scientific Films: 4 (J. and P. Wegner).
Planet Earth Pictures: 14-15 (Geoff Du Feu), 24 (Steve Bloom).
Franklin Watts Photo Library: 26-27.

Printed in Hong Kong

1 2 3 4 5 6 7 8 9 06 05 04 03 02

TAILS

Written by
Nicola Whittaker

Gareth Stevens Publishing
A WORLD ALMANAC EDUCATION GROUP COMPANY

Different
creatures have

different
tails.

5

Some tails
have
scales.

6

Some tails have hair.

Some are **bushy.**

Some are
bare.

Some tails are **short**.

13

Some tails
are **long**.

14

Some tails
are **curly**.

Some tails smell **strong**!

Some tails
can
wag.

18

Some tails can

can

cling.

Some tails

rattle.

Some tails

22

Some tails **swim**.

Some tails have **eyes**.

My tail is **missing**.

I wonder **why**!

Featured

Parakeet
Bird (parrot family)
Lives: Australia
Eats: seeds
Lives in huge flocks
in the wild.

Ring-Tailed Lemur
Mammal (lemur family)
Lives: Madagascar
Eats: plants
Travels with its tail raised to
keep its group together.

Siamese Fighting Fish
Fish (labyrinth fish family)
Lives: Southeast Asia
Eats: insects
Males attack each other and
fight when they get too close.

Horse
Mammal (horse family)
Lives: worldwide
Eats: grass
Uses its tail like a flyswatter
to brush away insects.

Creatures

Red Squirrel
Mammal (squirrel family)
Lives: Europe and Asia
Eats: nuts and seeds
Uses its tail to shelter itself
from cold winds and rain.

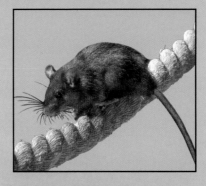

Black Rat
Mammal (rat/mouse family)
Lives: once worldwide, now rare
Eats: almost anything
Its scaly tail is longer than the
total length of its head and body.

Bobcat
Mammal (cat family)
Lives: North America
Eats: rabbits and rodents
Gets its name from its
stubby tail.

Emperor Dragonfly
Insect (dragonfly family)
Lives: Europe, Asia, and Africa
Eats: insects
Cannot fold its wings like
other flying insects.

29

Featured

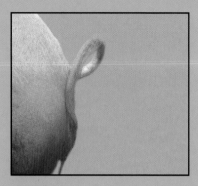

Pig
Mammal (pig family)
Lives: worldwide
Eats: almost anything
Raised as a farm animal
for thousands of years.

Striped Skunk
Mammal (skunk family)
Lives: North America
Eats: mice and insects
Raises its tail and squirts a
smelly liquid when alarmed.

Bull Terrier
Mammal (dog family)
Lives: worldwide
Eats: pet foods
Can be a playful, loyal pet
but needs strict training.

Flap-Necked Chameleon
Reptile (lizard family)
Lives: South Africa
Eats: insects
Can use its prehensile tail as
a fifth leg for climbing.

Creatures

Rattlesnake
Reptile (snake family)
Lives: North and South America
Eats: small animals and eggs
Rattles the tip of its tail to warn
and scare away enemies.

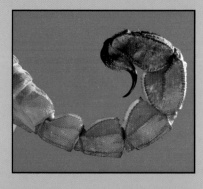

Fat-Tailed Scorpion
Arachnid (spider/scorpion family)
Lives: North Africa
Eats: insects
Defends itself and kills prey with
its poisonous sting.

Bottlenose Dolphin
Mammal (dolphin family)
Lives: all seas except polar
Eats: fish and squid
Uses its powerful tail fins
to swim and to jump.

Peacock
Bird (pheasant family)
Lives: Asia
Eats: seeds, insects, and plants
Male fans out its colorful tail
feathers to attract females.

Index

(**Boldface** entries indicate pictures.)